MW00676277

Brigitte Corell

A Gift For You

Great ideas for
quick and easy
handmade gifts

CHILDRENS PRESS ®
CHICAGO

For Dino and Ida

Translation by Mrs. Werner Lippmann and Mrs. Ruth Bookey
Cover, illustrations, and organization by Brigitte Corell
Cover photo and interior photos by Dagfinn Sivertsen
Photos on pages 11, 15, 25, 39 by Bernhard Hageman

Library of Congress Cataloging-in-Publication Data

Corell, Brigitte.
    [Schenk ich dir. English]
    A gift for you / by Brigitte Corell.
        p. cm.
    Translation of: Das Schenk ich dir.
    Includes index.
    Summary: Gives instructions for making a variety of simple items
        to give as gifts.
    ISBN 0-516-09260-X
    1. Handicraft—Juvenile literature. [1. Handicraft. 2 Gifts.]
        I. Title.
TT160.C67513 1992
745.5—dc20   91-44377
                                                            CIP
                                                             AC

Published in the United States in 1992 by Childrens Press®, Inc.
5440 North Cumberland Avenue, Chicago, IL 60656

Copyright © 1992, 1988 by Ravensburger Buchverlag Otto Maier GmbH
Germany. Originally published in Germany under the title
Das schenk ich dir.

1 2 3 4 5 6 7 8 9 0 R 01 00 99 98 97 96 95 94 93 92

Contents

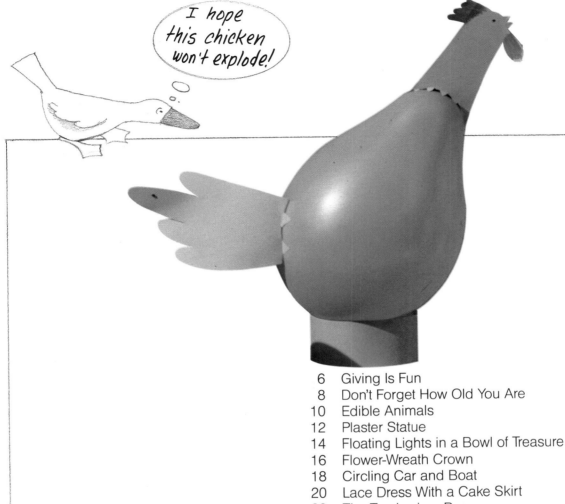

Giving Is Fun

It's fun to make presents.
It's even more fun to make funny presents.
It's the most fun of all to make unusual presents
that cost next to nothing.

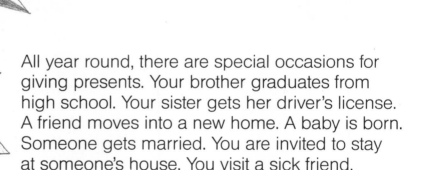

I love
funny-looking birds
the most.

All year round, there are special occasions for giving presents. Your brother graduates from high school. Your sister gets her driver's license. A friend moves into a new home. A baby is born. Someone gets married. You are invited to stay at someone's house. You visit a sick friend. It's Mother's Day.

A handmade gift costs less and means more than a gift you can buy in a store. A handmade gift is specially created for a special person. In this book there are sixty gift ideas. Most of the materials are things you may already have around the house. Some can be found outdoors. The other materials are easy to find and don't cost a lot. You'll use such things as paper, boxes, old newspapers, glue, paints, felt-tip markers, crayons, plaster of paris, and crepe paper.

If you don't already have a scrap box, start one. In it you can save little boxes, toilet-paper rolls, paper plates, cardboard, gift wrappings, pinecones, shells, and lots more. You do not need any special talent to do the projects in this book. You just need a little time. And the finished projects do not have to look exactly like the pictures in this book. The ones you make might even look better.

In the following pages, you will find ideas for all kinds of gifts for all kinds of people. You may want to write a poem to go with your gift.

There are more ideas in the "Extra Tips." Some of these "extras" can be made at the last minute. If you would like to make a colorful cardboard cake like the one shown above, you'll probably enjoy the other projects in this book.

I'm only interested in the Extra Tips!

Don't Forget How Old You Are

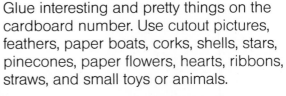

I collected
all this stuff
during the year.

How to Do It:

Draw the number of the birthday child's age on a piece of cardboard and cut out the number.

1

You could wrap colored crepe-paper strips around the number, or paint it.

2

Glue interesting and pretty things on the cardboard number. Use cutout pictures, feathers, paper boats, corks, shells, stars, pinecones, paper flowers, hearts, ribbons, straws, and small toys or animals.

Below: How to cut out stars, hearts, and palm leaves.

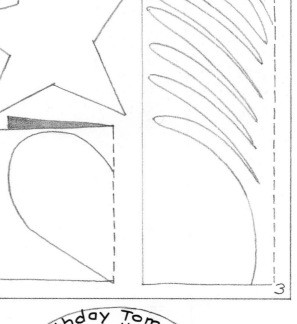

3

I'm getting dizzy reading this.

Extra Tip

An unusual birthday card

Draw the number of the birthday on cardboard and cut out the number. Write good wishes all over and all around the number. Or draw little faces all over. Or do you have other ideas?

Happy Birthday Tom – congratulations – Now you are 8 years old! Have a good day – I hope all your wishes come true! Now you are one year older!

A mouse and a bird
go bananas.

Fruit animals look
good enough to eat—
and they are!

Edible Animals

How to Do It:

Cut bananas and
use the pieces
to make noses,
heads, necks, or tails.

1

To make a
stand, glue
the ends of a
cardboard
strip together
to form a circle.

2

Use toothpicks
to connect the
fruit pieces.

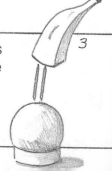

3

Break toothpicks in half to attach berry eyes.

Use 2 toothpicks to attach large pieces of fruit.

4

5

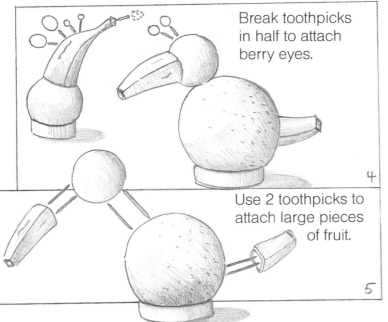

Quick! Buy more bananas!

Extra Tip

Banana-peel boat

Open a banana carefully on the concave side. Take out the fruit without damaging the peel. Cut the fruit in half and set the halves in the banana-peel "boat." Use cloves for the eyes and noses, and 4 toothpicks as oars. (The oars help the boat to stand.)

You deserve a statue!

Plaster Statue

I'd like to put a statue of you in the park. But first I'll make a miniature statue of you!

How to Do It:

1 Glue a photo onto cardboard and cut the photo out.

2 Glue the figure to a stick.

3 Mix plaster of paris in a plastic bowl. Use 2 parts plaster to 1 part water.

4 Pour plaster into an empty plastic or cardboard container.

5 When the container is full, smooth out the top.

6 Push the stick into the wet plaster.

7 When the plaster is hard (in about 30 minutes), cut the container and peel it off. Glue a little umbrella on the "statue." If you don't have a small paper umbrella, here is how you can make one:

Use a piece of paper and a toothpick.

Extra Tip

Permanent handprint

Pour wet plaster into the cover of an old box. Smooth out the plaster. Before it dries, press your hand into the plaster. Let the plaster dry a little under your hand. Then lift your hand off slowly to keep the print clear.

Lights show the way to
sunken treasure.

Floating Lights in a Bowl of Treasure

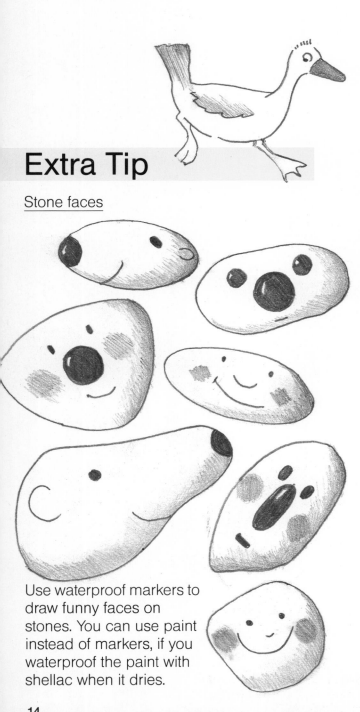

Extra Tip

<u>Stone faces</u>

Use waterproof markers to
draw funny faces on
stones. You can use paint
instead of markers, if you
waterproof the paint with
shellac when it dries.

How to Do It:

Paint some stones with bright
colors. When the paint is dry,
add a coat of shellac.

When the shellac is dry, put
the stones in a glass bowl
and fill the bowl with water.

Set votive candles
on the water to float.

Extra Tip

<u>Candle boats</u>

Cut small boat shapes out of Styrofoam
(you can also use bark). Glue a votive candle
on the boats. Instead of glue you can
use tape—or drip some melted wax
onto the surface of the boat, then
press the votive candle into the
wet wax and let the wax dry.

Through the
dark night sails
my floating
light.

We see flowers
everywhere.
You can braid them
for your hair.

Flower-Wreath Crown

How to Do It:

Extra Tip

A prize for the winner

Fresh bay leaves glued onto a strip of
cardboard make a great "laurel wreath."
You can paint the wreath with gold paint
or decorate it with leaves cut out of
gold foil.

Circling Car
and Boat

A record without music?
Put it on the
turntable anyway.

How to Do It:

1

Cut out a
quarter circle from
construction paper and
glue it together to form a cone.

2

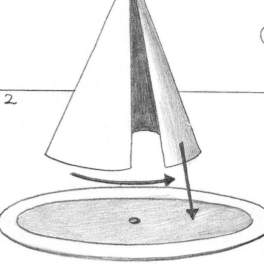

Cut a stiff cardboard circle the size
of a long-playing record. Paint the
circle or cover it with colored paper.

3

Paint scenery (a
landscape and
sky) on the cone.
Glue on paper
clouds so that
they stick out
from the cone.

4

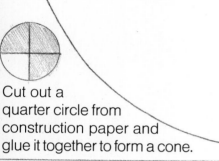

To make the plane:
Fold a piece of paper.
Draw and cut out the
plane's body. (Do not
cut through the top of
the fold.) Draw on
windows, and cut slits
for the wing. Cut out
the wing and slide it
through the slits.

5

Cut a hole in the upper part of the
cone and stick a flexible straw in the
hole. Tape the plane onto the end of
the straw. Put the finished construction
on a stereo turntable.

How to fold a boat:

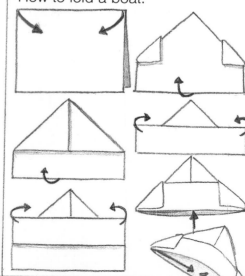

Glue the name of your friend on
a plastic strip. Glue the strip of
plastic into the tail of the plane.

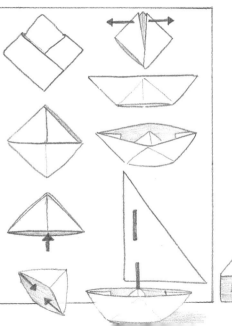

Extra Tip

Optical illusion

Paint wide diagonal stripes on a piece of heavy paper. Glue the paper together to form a cylinder. Place the cylinder on the turntable. As the turntable turns, the colored lines will keep moving up endlessly.

A dressed-up cake
for a special day

This elegant lady
wears a
delicious dress!

Lace Dress With a Cake Skirt

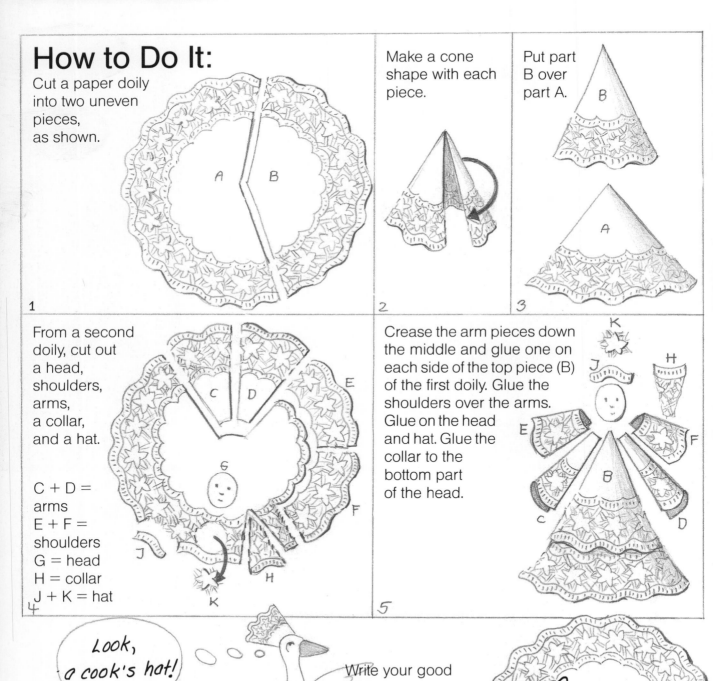

How to Do It:

Cut a paper doily into two uneven pieces, as shown.

1

Make a cone shape with each piece.

2

Put part B over part A.

3

From a second doily, cut out a head, shoulders, arms, a collar, and a hat.

C + D = arms
E + F = shoulders
G = head
H = collar
J + K = hat

4

Crease the arm pieces down the middle and glue one on each side of the top piece (B) of the first doily. Glue the shoulders over the arms. Glue on the head and hat. Glue the collar to the bottom part of the head.

5

Look, a cook's hat!

Extra Tip

Paper-doily congratulations

Write your good wishes or congratulations in the middle of a paper doily. Then put it into an envelope.

Congratulations ♡ from Toby and Sophie

For world travelers
and couch potatoes

The Tropics in a Box

It's exciting to travel
And great fun to roam,
But all journeys end
And there's no place like home.

Extra Tip

Minipicture in a minibox

Cut out little pictures. Travel advertisements for foreign lands often include small pictures that would fit in a matchbox. Maybe you can find small people or animals among your own toys. Use your imagination!

How to Do It:

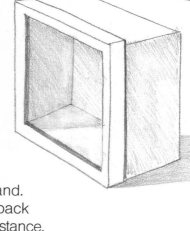

1 Cut a big window into the cover of a box. Keep a ¾-inch (2-cm) border. Stand the box on its side with the window in front. Spread glue on the back wall of the box and sprinkle on sand. When the glue dries, pour off the excess sand. Paint a scene on the back wall—sky or water, for instance.

2 Cut the top off a pineapple and stick the top into an empty toilet-paper roll. Fasten with 2 straight pins. Glue the pineapple tree in the box.

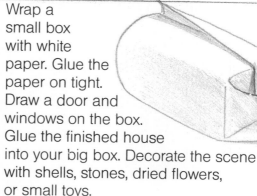

3 Wrap a small box with white paper. Glue the paper on tight. Draw a door and windows on the box. Glue the finished house into your big box. Decorate the scene with shells, stones, dried flowers, or small toys.

Extra Tip

Another scene

Cut out pictures of faraway places. Magazines and calendars are good sources. The background pictures can be glued directly onto the back of the box. Any figures in the front should be glued on cardboard and cut out, leaving a "foot" that can be glued into place as shown. (Figures can be trees, people, houses, animals, and so on.)

Flowers for Sweet Berries

How to Do It:

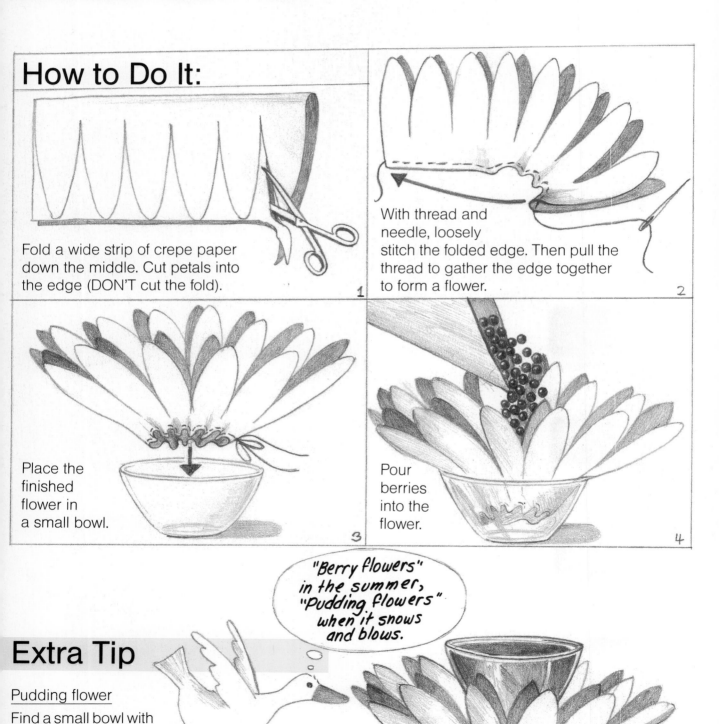

1 Fold a wide strip of crepe paper down the middle. Cut petals into the edge (DON'T cut the fold).

2 With thread and needle, loosely stitch the folded edge. Then pull the thread to gather the edge together to form a flower.

3 Place the finished flower in a small bowl.

4 Pour berries into the flower.

"Berry flowers" in the summer, "Pudding flowers" when it snows and blows.

Extra Tip

Pudding flower

Find a small bowl with pudding and set it in the flower.

24

Catch the wind.

Windsock

How to Do It:

Cut letters, dots, stars, or hearts out of tissue paper. Glue the cutouts onto a large, clear-plastic bag. (Dry-cleaner bags are good for this.) Make a ring out of wire, fold the plastic bag over the wire and tape it securely.

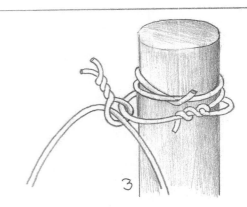

Attach the finished windsock to a pole with wire, so that the sock can sway in the wind and turn when the wind changes direction. Illustrations 3 and 4 show how to attach your windsock.

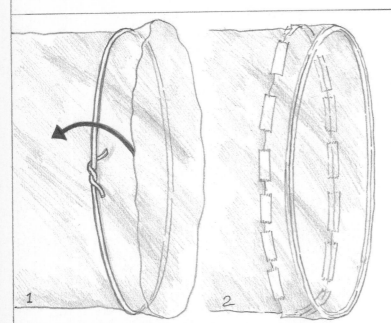

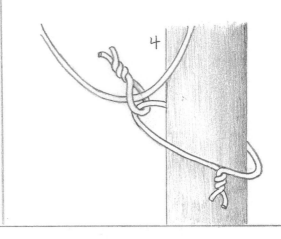

Fold about 2 inches (5 cm) of the windsock over the wire. Use clear tape to attach the plastic securely.

Extra Tip

Windy gift

Cut strips of crepe paper of different lengths and colors. Attach the strips to the end of a pole.

For shy hens
and sly geese

These happy feathered
friends will peck
the crumbs you dropped
during the party.

Blown-Up
Poultry?

How to Do It:

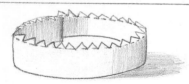

Cut narrow and wide strips of poster
board. Cut zigzags on one side of
each strip. Glue strips together into
rings. Blow up a balloon. If the
balloon isn't round, the bird can sit
straight up or sideways. Glue the
balloon on the stand.

Draw
heads and tails on cardboard. Draw zigzags on the ends...

Extra Tip

<u>Hidden present</u>
Carefully pull the open end
of a balloon over a small toy.
Then blow up the balloon
and knot it to keep
the air in. Now the
gift is hidden
in a balloon.

and cut them out.
Bend the zigzags alternately in and out.
Glue on the balloon.

For chocolate lovers

Chocolate-Covered Fruit

Do you think these fruits grew on a tree? Or did they come to you from the Land of Fantasy?

How to Do It:

1 Push fruit onto a pointed stick.

2 Ask an adult to help you. Melt semisweet chocolate or chocolate bits over low heat, stirring constantly.

3 Spoon melted chocolate onto fruit (over a bowl) turning fruit as you spoon chocolate.

Fill a large glass or pottery jar with sand or small stones. Tie a ribbon around the jar. A flowerpot can be used for this, too.

4 Before the chocolate hardens, turn the fruit as you pour on nuts, and/or candy sprinkles.

5 Place the fruits in the jar like flowers.

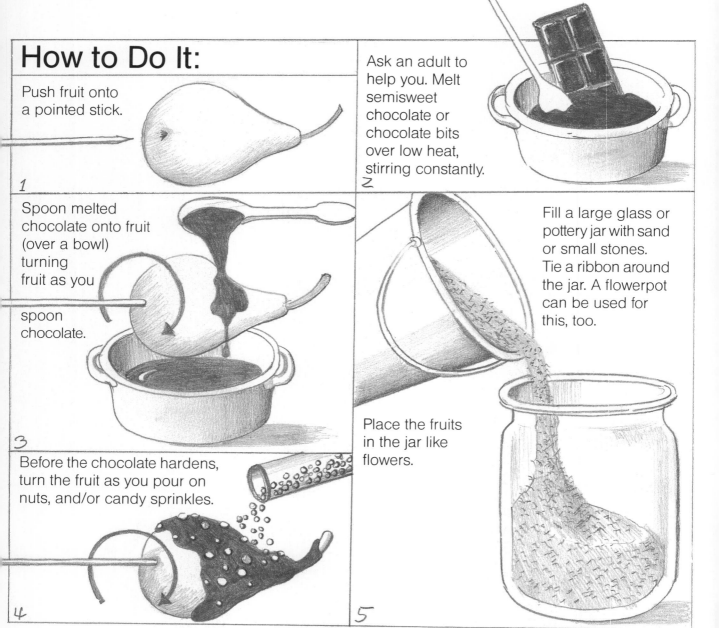

Aromatic Balls

Stick cloves close together into an unpeeled orange. The orange smells wonderful, and it can be used as a decoration in a fruit bowl or for a table.

Extra Tip

For sugar detectives
and cake inspectors

Many cakes are so beautiful
that it seems a shame to eat
them. This cake cannot be
eaten at all!

A Fake, But Sweet Cake

How to Do It:

Cut small zigzags on one side of a cardboard
strip. Glue the strip together to form a ring.
Bend the zigzags toward the inside, and
glue on a circle of cardboard to cover the
ring. The second layer of the cake is made
the same way, only a bit smaller.

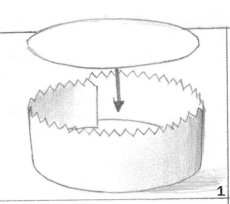

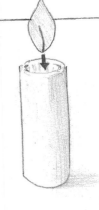

Wrap each layer of the cake in crepe paper.
Fold the extra paper over the cake, and glue it
down with a circle of cardboard. Glue the layers
together. Decorate your cake with the candles,
paper flowers, and ribbons. Put a name on the
cake if you want.

For candles, use
empty toilet-paper
rolls wrapped with
crepe paper. Cut a
flame shape out of
yellow tissue paper
and paint a wick
on the flame. Glue
the flame to the
inside of the roll.
Decorate the cake
with paper flowers
(see page 42).

(see page 42).

Extra Tip

Send a piece of cake in the mail!

Pieces of cake to send away

Draw a picture of a piece of cake
on heavy paper or light cardboard.
Put it in an envelope and mail it to
a friend. Or glue it together, fill it
with nuts or candy, and then mail it.

Advertise your name
(or a friend's name) with lights.

I just had a bright idea.
Here it is:

Your Name
in
Lights

How to Do It:

For each letter, you will need a milk carton with the top cut off.

Glue black or white paper around the milk carton.

Draw a letter on each carton and carefully cut out the letter.

Glue a different color of tissue paper behind each cutout letter.

Stand the letters beside each other on a windowsill. Put a small flashlight behind each letter. (If you want, you could cut the letter on the other side too, so that the name will show on both sides.)

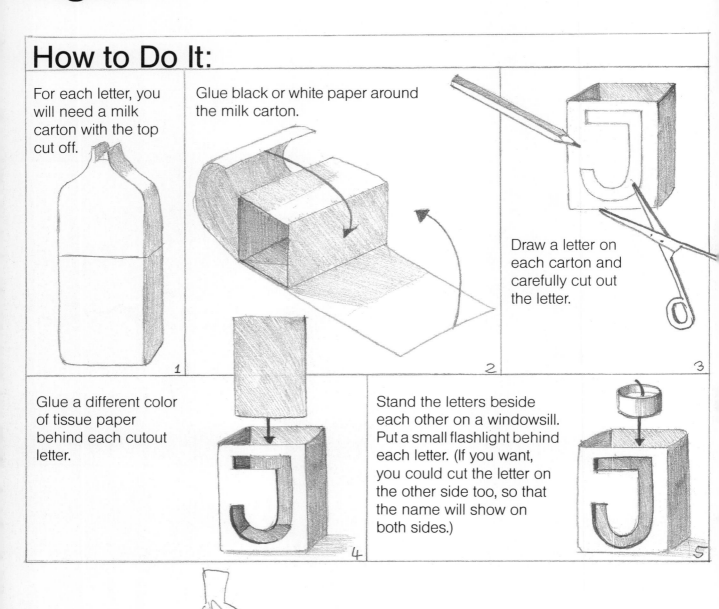

Extra Tip

Magic light dots
You can simply punch out letters or numbers with a nail!
Then you won't need the tissue paper.

For daydreamers and builders
of castles in the air

I had quite a time finding
the right stuff!

Dreams for You

How to Do It:

Cut pictures out of catalogs and
magazines. Glue them on cardboard,
then cut them out again. Cover a box
with pretty paper. Put all the pictures
into the box. It will make an
interesting gift.

Extra Tip

Last-minute gift idea:
A coupon

Find pictures in magazines and
newspapers to use as coupons. For
example, a picture of a wild animal
can be a coupon for a zoo visit.
A picture of real jewelry can be
a coupon for a handmade necklace.
You can give a coupon to invite
a friend for an ice-cream sundae or
a homemade cake. You can probably
find many pictures of cakes, cookies,
and other goodies.

Invitation
to an
Ice-Cream
Sundae

A shaggy-haired pot

Wild-Grass Head

Flowers fade quickly, but the hair in this pot will stay green a long time.

How to Do It:

Paint a face on a flowerpot.

1

Using felt-tip markers or paint, make eyes, a nose, and a mouth.

2

Dig up a clump of long grass or weeds along with some soil…

3

…and plant it in the pot.

4

Find a plant stand, or staple some boxes together to make a stand.

5

Cover the stand with a tablecloth. Place the pot on top. Put it outdoors or on your porch or deck. It will add a touch of humor.

6

I'd like to eat those seeds.

Water this, don't forget! You'll get some plants yet.

Extra Tip

For city gardeners

City gardeners could put some soil in the flowerpot, plant some seeds, then set the pot in a sunny place and water it.

Special Scene for a Special Person

How to Do It:

Cut a window into a box cover. Glue colored paper to the inside of the box, or paint it. Cut slits in each side of the box, and push a long, narrow cardboard strip through the slits.

Paint curtains on the theater, or make curtains out of cloth or paper and glue them on.

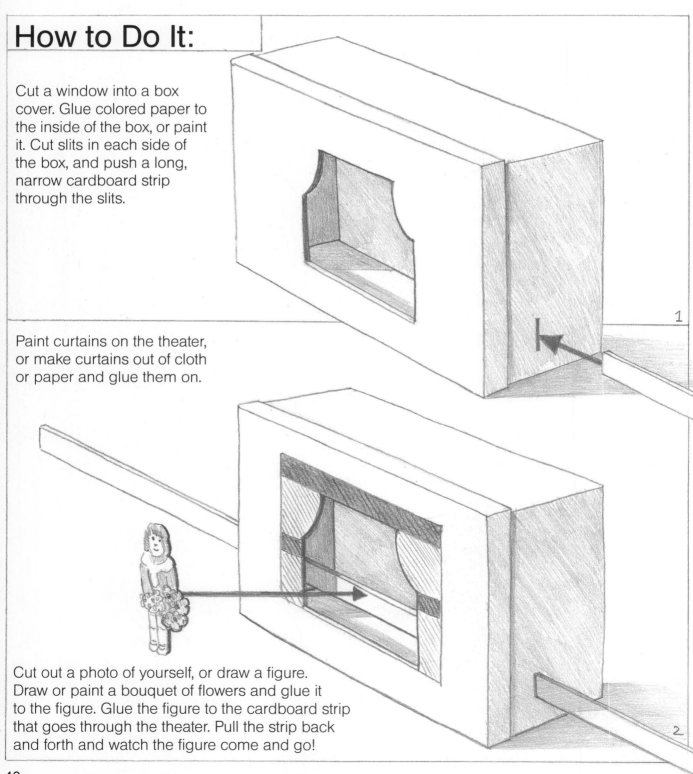

Cut out a photo of yourself, or draw a figure. Draw or paint a bouquet of flowers and glue it to the figure. Glue the figure to the cardboard strip that goes through the theater. Pull the strip back and forth and watch the figure come and go!

Extra Tip

Wrap colorful paper around the bottom
of your picture and glue the paper to the
back. Cut a slit in the middle. Draw or paint
a bouquet of flowers. Glue the cutout
bouquet to a cardboard stick. Then you
can move the bouquet up and down.

Royal Crown and Collar

A crown can make you a king or queen.

How to Do It:

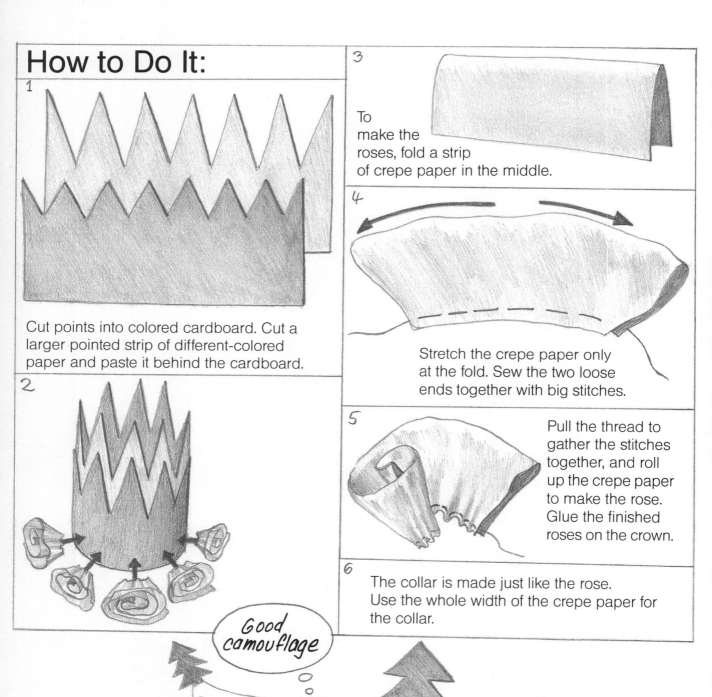

1 Cut points into colored cardboard. Cut a larger pointed strip of different-colored paper and paste it behind the cardboard.

2

3 To make the roses, fold a strip of crepe paper in the middle.

4 Stretch the crepe paper only at the fold. Sew the two loose ends together with big stitches.

5 Pull the thread to gather the stitches together, and roll up the crepe paper to make the rose. Glue the finished roses on the crown.

6 The collar is made just like the rose. Use the whole width of the crepe paper for the collar.

Good camouflage

Extra Tip

A crown for forest explorers and nature lovers

Glue the ends of a paper strip together to form a circle. Draw a tree, then cut out the tree and glue it to the circle.

For animal friends
and dog lovers

Cake
Watchdogs

Nobody will steal
this cake—
because it's
well guarded!

How to Do It:

Fold two pieces of cardboard, about
5 inches by 11 inches (12 x 28 cm) in the
middle. Paint a dog on the cardboard
and cut it out. (Don't cut the top fold.)

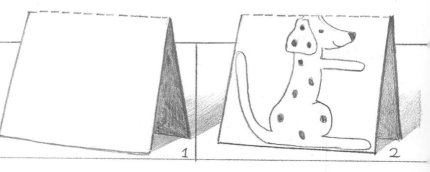

Paint the dog on both sides. Spread its feet apart and set it on a rectangular paper or plastic plate. Cut a round piece of cardboard for the tray on the dog's paws. Glue the tray onto the paws.

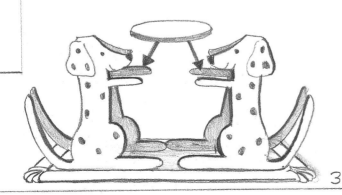

3

I'll stick to hot dogs with lots of mustard.

Extra Tip

Rectangular paper plates or trays make nice picture frames.

A long-lasting gift

A good present for
a special friend

Coupon Tree

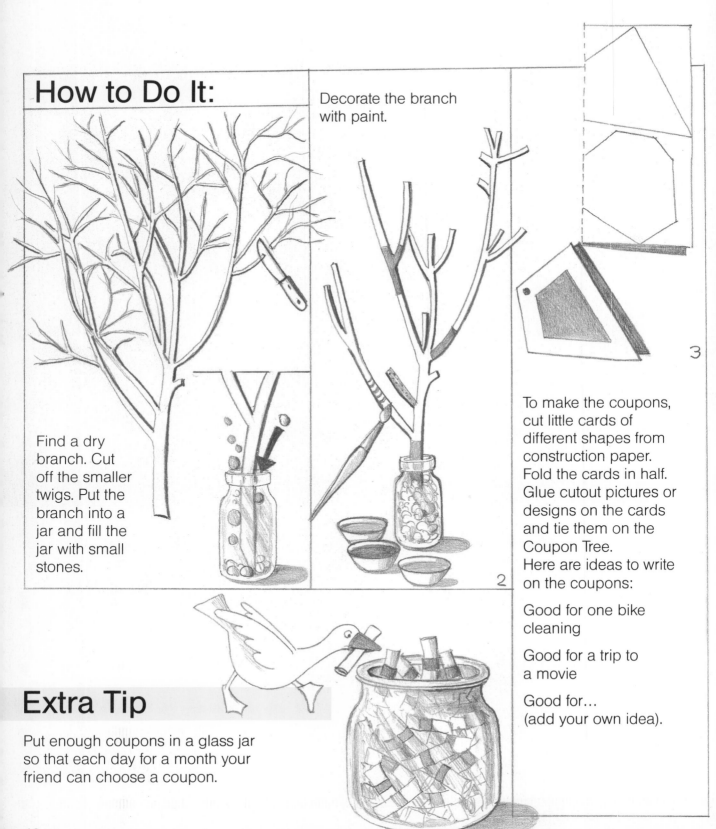

How to Do It:

Decorate the branch
with paint.

Find a dry
branch. Cut
off the smaller
twigs. Put the
branch into a
jar and fill the
jar with small
stones.

2

3

To make the coupons,
cut little cards of
different shapes from
construction paper.
Fold the cards in half.
Glue cutout pictures or
designs on the cards
and tie them on the
Coupon Tree.
Here are ideas to write
on the coupons:

Good for one bike
cleaning

Good for a trip to
a movie

Good for…
(add your own idea).

Extra Tip

Put enough coupons in a glass jar
so that each day for a month your
friend can choose a coupon.

46

Photo Cover for a Box of Photos

How to Do It:

Cover a box with colored paper. Cut a square, a circle, or an oval out of construction paper. Glue it to the cover of the box. Next, glue a photo on the construction paper.

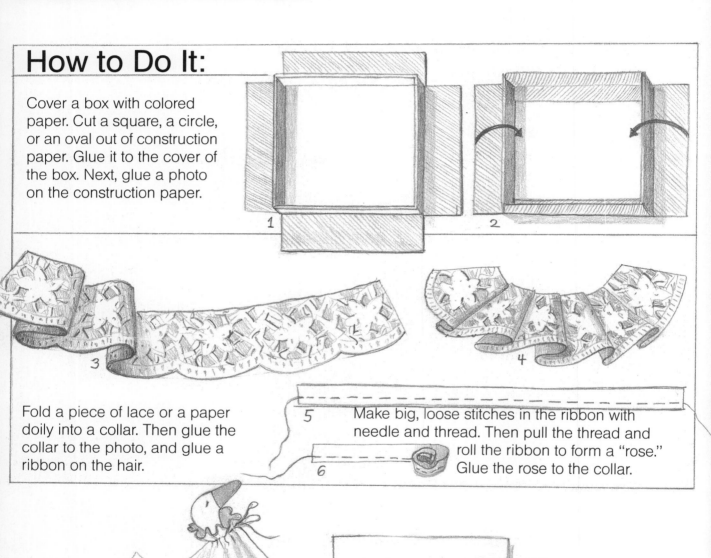

Fold a piece of lace or a paper doily into a collar. Then glue the collar to the photo, and glue a ribbon on the hair.

Make big, loose stitches in the ribbon with needle and thread. Then pull the thread and roll the ribbon to form a "rose." Glue the rose to the collar.

Extra Tip

Picture with cloth dress

Glue a photo on the cover of an oval box. Gather the top of a piece of cloth to make a dress, and glue the dress to the picture.

Pop-Concert Popcorn

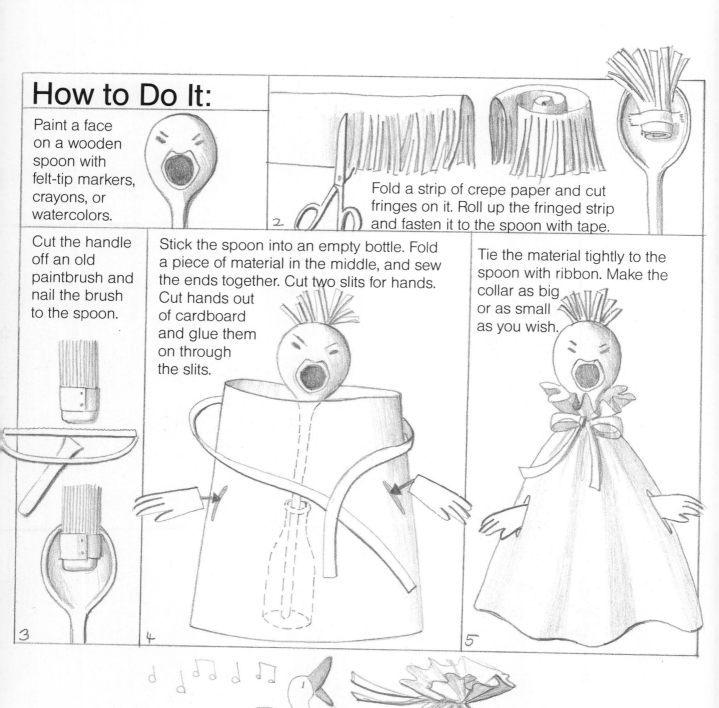

How to Do It:

Paint a face on a wooden spoon with felt-tip markers, crayons, or watercolors.

Fold a strip of crepe paper and cut fringes on it. Roll up the fringed strip and fasten it to the spoon with tape.

Cut the handle off an old paintbrush and nail the brush to the spoon.

Stick the spoon into an empty bottle. Fold a piece of material in the middle, and sew the ends together. Cut two slits for hands. Cut hands out of cardboard and glue them on through the slits.

Tie the material tightly to the spoon with ribbon. Make the collar as big or as small as you wish.

Pop popcorn in the microwave and serve.

Extra Tip

Hot rhythm on a hot pan

Surprise made by
busy hands

Surprise
in a
Yarn Ball

A present is hidden under
the yarn. But you must knit
something to unwind the
yarn to get the present.

How to Do It:

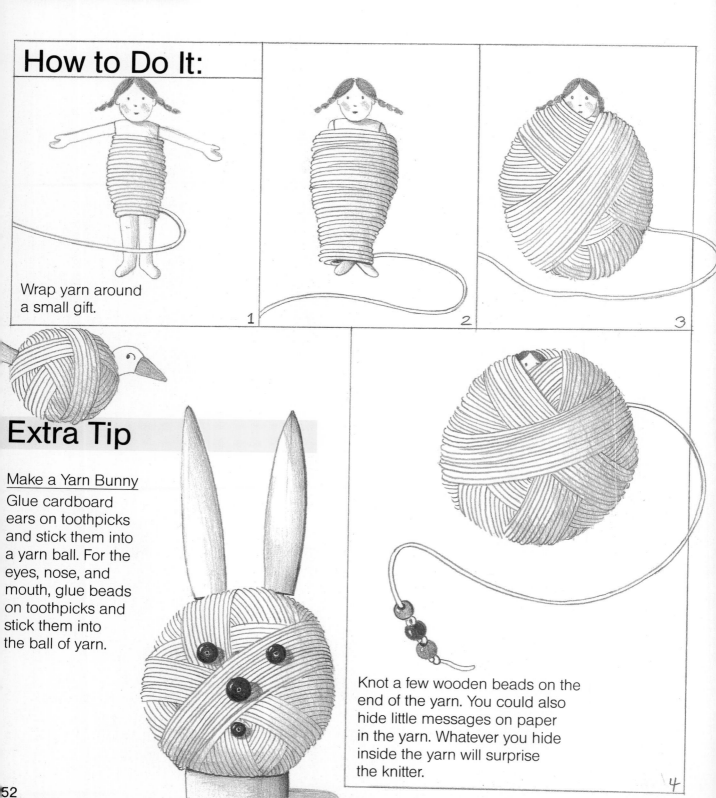

Wrap yarn around
a small gift.

1

2

3

Extra Tip

Make a Yarn Bunny
Glue cardboard
ears on toothpicks
and stick them into
a yarn ball. For the
eyes, nose, and
mouth, glue beads
on toothpicks and
stick them into
the ball of yarn.

Knot a few wooden beads on the
end of the yarn. You could also
hide little messages on paper
in the yarn. Whatever you hide
inside the yarn will surprise
the knitter.

4

For crowd lovers

Congratulations from a Fun Crowd

I've brought along a few friends, so you don't have to celebrate alone.

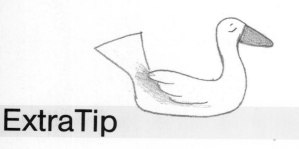

ExtraTip

Head-on-head pictures

Cut out lots of heads and glue them on cardboard. Be sure to include a photo of yourself among all those heads!

How to Do It:

Cut funny people and animals out of old magazines. Size makes no difference.

Glue a roughly cutout figure on cardboard. Draw a rectangle below the feet as shown.

1

Now carefully cut around the outline of the figure.

2

Make a cut between the feet at the bottom of the cardboard rectangle. Bend one half back and the other forward, as shown. Glue the figure to a little wooden board or a piece of heavy cardboard.

3

If the figure is too shaky, glue a triangle of cardboard on the back.

4

Nature's Vase

This bouquet was gathered
in the forest and
on the meadow.

How to Do It:

1 Cut the top off a melon or a pumpkin.

2 Remove the pulp with a big spoon. You can eat the pulp if it's a melon, or cook it if it's a pumpkin.

3 Use a big nail or a screwdriver to make holes in the upper half of the fruit.

4 Put flowers or leaves in the vase and through some of the holes.

ExtraTip
Orange lamps
Cut the tops off some oranges and hollow out
the insides. (Save the fruit for a salad.) Put a
votive candle in each orange. These lamps look
beautiful if you set them in the snow.

Painting without paint

Wrapping-Paper Art

You don't need paint and brushes to make a colorful picture. All you need is a pair of scissors.

How to Do It:

Don't throw away wrapping paper after unwrapping presents. It's great for cutting and pasting collages. The picture on the right side was made from cut-up wrapping paper, even the eyes, ears, nose, and mouth.

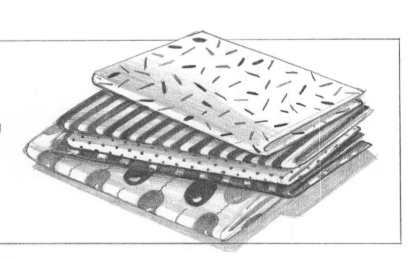

Extra Tip

Memory game
Glue wrapping paper on cardboard squares. Always make two of the same pattern. Write a different number on the back of each square and line them up on the table, number side up. Pick two numbers and turn over those squares to see if you have a match (if not, put them back, number side up). Continue until all the squares have been matched.

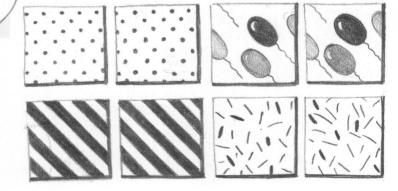

Extra Tip

Picture dominoes
Glue two squares of different wrapping paper on cardboard rectangles side by side as shown. Make sure that each domino has a matching pattern on another domino.

Jewelry doesn't always have
to be gold or silver.

This jewelry can
look very real.

Plastic Straw Jewelry

How to Do It:

Cut plastic straws into even pieces. Thread
a needle on each end of the thread. Join the
straw pieces as shown. The first straw piece
goes in the center of the thread.

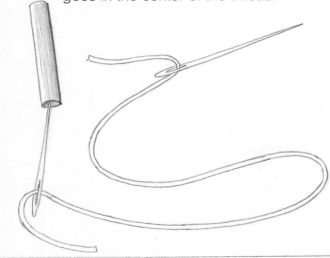

Through each
straw, put threaded
needles going in
opposite directions.

1

2

Pull tightly on both thread ends, so that the second
piece of straw is right next to the first piece.
Continue adding
straw pieces until
the bracelet
or piece of
jewelry is the
length you wish.

Then put both
needles in
opposite
directions
through the
first piece
and knot.

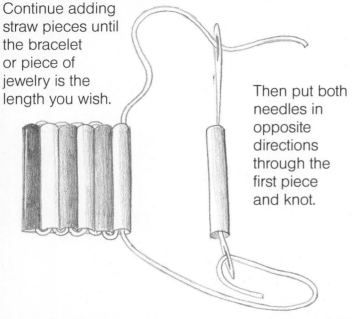

To make the red necklace, cut pieces
of different lengths. Thread as shown in
the picture.

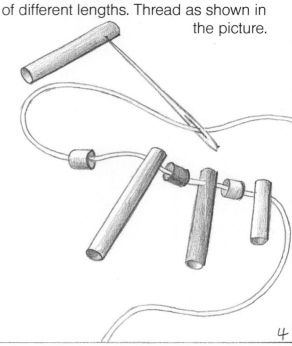

3

4

I'll build myself a colorful house.

Extra Tip

Straw pictures

You can make pictures by gluing colored plastic straws to paper in various designs. Glue the design on transparent paper and hang it in front of a sunny window.

All your ducks
in a row

A lot of quacking
and wing-beating
for you today

Dancing
Beak-to-Beak

How to Do It:

1

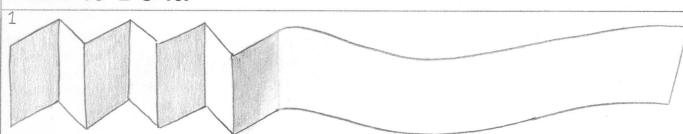

Fold a long piece of paper in accordion pleats.

2

Draw a duck on the top fold. Make sure the tail and beak touch the edges. (See pattern on page 63.)

3

Cut the duck out, cutting through all the folds together. Do not cut through the tips of the beak and tail. If you can't get the scissors to cut, make two thinner stacks and then join the strips of ducks with tape.

4

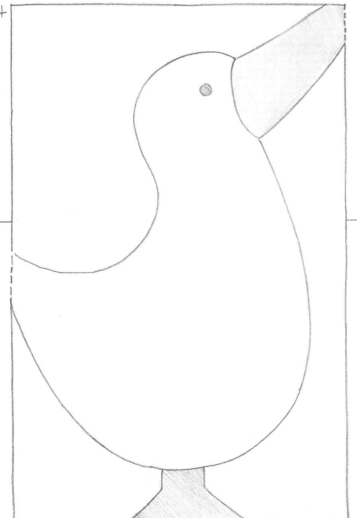

Pattern for the dancing ducks: The tips of the beak and the tail must be on the folded edges.

Extra Tip

<u>For decoration</u>
Fold a paper strip in accordion pleats. Then cut out patterns. Open the strip and glue the ends together. Put the strip around a flowerpot, a small flashlight, or a bottle for a gift.

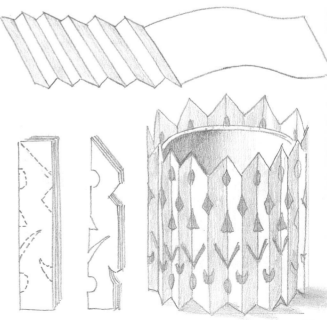

Index